THE HOSPITAL

The Inside Story

Contents

Welcome to the hospital!

My name is Christle Nwora and I am a doctor. I knew I wanted to practice medicine from a young age. My mother is a nurse and I loved flipping through her medical textbooks as a child. I was curious about how the human body works and what happens when certain parts of the body break down. As I grew up, I also became interested in why some groups of people had better health than others.

I would have loved this book as a child! It's a story set over the course of one day at a busy hospital. As you turn the pages, you'll meet all of the incredible people who work together to keep everyone healthy—from surgeons and café staff to nurses and cleaners.

Going to a hospital—either to visit someone or for treatment yourself—can be scary. My hope is that reading this book will help you better understand what goes on inside a hospital and why it happens. As well as explaining the different jobs people do, this book will explain some of the science behind the medical techniques used in hospitals.

Today I work as a resident physician at Johns Hopkins Hospital in Baltimore, Maryland. A resident physician is a doctor who has finished medical school and is in a special training program. Every day I'm learning how to provide the best care for adults and children! It's an amazing job and no two days are ever the same. I work alongside wonderful doctors and other health professionals with the goal of providing excellent care to our patients.

Next time you find yourself at a doctor's office or in a hospital waiting room, use this book to see if you can identify the different types of jobs going on around you. It might even inspire you to work in a hospital yourself one day...

Dr. Christle Nwora

A beacon in the night

Before the sun rises and the birds start to sing, there's one place in the city that is wide awake. Darkness cloaks the sleeping buildings, but among them a beacon of light is visible for miles around—welcome to the hospital!

You never know when someone might feel ill or have an accident, so the people who work in the hospital have to be prepared for anything. The hospital is open at all hours of the day, and the talented people inside keep it bright even on the darkest of nights.

The hospital is a place where people come for all kinds of help. From people with broken bones to expectant parents, the hospital welcomes anyone in need. The incredible people who work here are kind and dedicated to helping people feel better. And they have a long day ahead!

Arriving in reception

At eight o'clock in the morning, Tess and Omari arrive at the hospital. Earlier Tess felt a strong squeeze in her belly and felt a little strange. She's nine months pregnant with her second child. Omari called the hospital and they were told to come in—Tess was going into labor! On the drive to the hospital, Tess breathed heavily while Omari tried to help her relax by playing calming music on the radio.

Once at the hospital, the couple make their way to the front desk. Slung over Omari's shoulder is a bag for Tess containing the things she will need once their baby is born. They answer a few questions and are guided toward an elevator that will take them to the maternity ward.

Feeding a hungry hospital

The kitchen is one of the busiest places in the hospital, especially at breakfast time. All the patients need something delicious to eat, and Head Chef Trini and her team work hard to make sure that the food is healthy and nutritious. Patients in their hospital rooms can pick from a menu, order a meal, and have it delivered right to them!

At the same time in the cafeteria, family members and hospital workers buzz around, buying food and coffee from the friendly staff. This is one of the places in the hospital where anyone can meet up with friends and discuss important news from the day. Dr. Joanna fills up her tray with breakfast to enjoy before heading off to check on her patients, while Tess and Omari's family grab a bite to eat as they wait for updates on how Tess is doing.

Breakfast in bed

It's Jesse's second day in the hospital and he's excited as his breakfast arrives from the kitchen. Yesterday he had a high temperature, and when he tried to play with his cousins, he quickly tired and preferred to take a nap. Jesse's mom was worried he was sick, so she brought him to the hospital for some tests. He was admitted to the pediatric ward, which is the department where kids are looked after. Dr. Wardah decided to keep him there overnight. She's pleased to see Jesse is looking much better this morning.

What does everything do?

Every hospital room comes fully equipped with amazing tools and gadgets that can be used to treat all sorts of conditions, as well as monitor how a patient is doing. These are some common tools you will find in most hospital rooms.

Monitor

This screen displays important information about your health, such as how often your heart is beating.

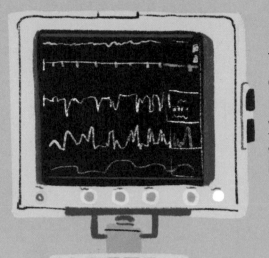

Drip

This bag holds important medication or fluids that help you feel better. They enter your body through a tube called an IV line.

Stethoscope

This tool allows doctors to listen to different sounds inside your body, like the sound of the breath in your lungs.

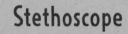

Blood pressure monitor

This tool wraps around your arm. It lets doctors know how well your heart is pumping blood around your body.

Hospital bed

The bed comes with different buttons that can move it up or down, or call a nurse for help.

A tour of the hospital

The hospital is divided into areas dedicated to different patients. Minh and his grandmother are reading in the sitting area of the pediatric ward, where Minh's younger sister is one of the children receiving treatment. Minh comes here with his grandmother and sister once a week, and all the nurses know his name. When he's older, Minh wants to be a nurse so he can help people who are unwell, just like his sister.

In the maternity ward, where new babies are born, Dr. Sven and his team are visiting each hospital room one by one. They do this once a day to check on their patients—this activity is called making rounds. The group is made up of doctors, nurses, and students.

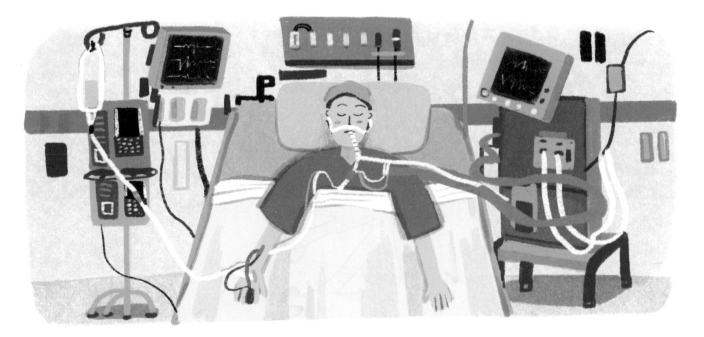

Sometimes people in the hospital are very sick and need a lot of care 24 hours a day. They are in a part of the hospital called the intensive care unit. People who work on this floor are trained to take care of the most critical patients.

Taking blood

Every morning, Maria receives a list of patients she has to visit that day. Maria is a phlebotomist (pronounced *fle-bot-omist*), which means she uses a needle to take blood from her patients. Many people—adults and kids—are afraid of needles, but Maria is a superstar at her job. She calms the patient before using the needle and gets just enough blood to run important tests to see what is wrong.

Maria has a special cart that she brings to each patient's room. It holds everything she needs to collect the samples for the laboratory tests. She has a colorful assortment of test tubes, bandages, and cleaning wipes. Maria also has labels for each patient, to make sure that their blood results go to the right doctor.

Today Maria is drawing blood from Lian, who hasn't been feeling well. Maria asks Lian to relax her hand and look at her mom. Maria counts to three and inserts the needle into Lian's arm. She collects the blood in a few test tubes, removes the needle, and places a bandage on Lian's arm.

"That wasn't so bad, was it?" she says, as she puts her tools back in her cart.

Phlebotomist

Phlebotomists are trained in carefully taking blood samples from patients.

Lab technician

Lab technicians perform different tests on samples of patient blood.

Pathologist

Pathologists are doctors trained to look at the blood test results and understand what they mean.

The testing team

When a doctor places an order for a special test involving taking a sample of blood, a phlebotomist like Maria gets a notification. They go to the bedside and draw the blood into a test tube. Then they deliver the sample to the laboratory, where it can be tested by scientists.

The cart

At any time of day or night you might spot a phlebotomist and their cart going down the hall. Because they don't know where they might be needed each day, they need to have all of their tools ready to go.

Phlebotomists use a special needle to draw blood from a patient.

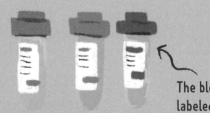

The blood is stored in labeled test tubes.

This band is tied around the arm. It makes it easier to see blood vessels—the tubes that transport blood around the body.

The lab

The laboratory where the tests take place is called the pathology lab. Dr. Rohan is looking at blood through a microscope. Later he will update the doctor who requested the test on the results. The information gathered from this lab helps guide the care for patients in the hospital.

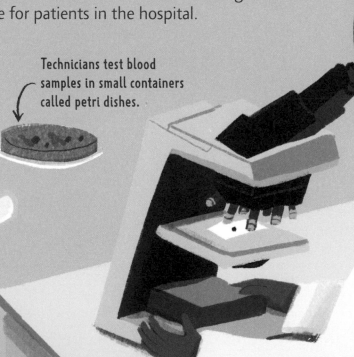

Slides are put under a microscope to see blood samples up close.

Technicians test blood samples in small containers called petri dishes.

You squeeze a pipette to transfer liquid from one place to another.

A trip to the clinic

Not all doctors work at the hospital—some are based at the nearby primary care clinic. This is where you can see a doctor if you are feeling well and need a routine checkup, or if you are feeling just a little bit under the weather. Sometimes your doctor will send you to the hospital for more treatment.

Today Rosie has come to the clinic with her dads (and her rabbit, Mr. Ears) for a checkup. Dr. Maya is pleased with Rosie's health—and just to be safe, she gives Mr. Ears a thorough examination too.

In a different room of the clinic, Aaron sits with Dr. Raheem. Aaron has been feeling very sad lately. He has found it difficult to wake up because he is always tired, and he does not have the energy to do the things he once enjoyed, like baking or walking his dogs.

Aaron has depression, and he sees Dr. Raheem every few months to discuss his feelings and what treatments he could take to make him feel better. Dr. Raheem is a psychiatrist (pronounced *sy-kya-trist*) and specializes in helping people improve their mental health.

An exciting wait

Terrence keeps his grandson Justin occupied as they wait for the arrival of the newest member of their family. The doctors have told them it is almost time for Tess and Omari's baby to be born! Grandma June is distracting herself from worrying by chatting with a friendly stranger who is waiting for her sister to give birth. Terrence is excited—all of his family have been born in this hospital, so he has very fond memories of this waiting room.

Justin is only two. He's old enough to realize that something special is happening, but too young to understand that he will have a new sibling very soon. For now, he's enjoying playing with his grandpa and the exciting collection of toys he's found hidden around the room.

Inside the delivery room, Tess and Omari are growing anxious. Their nurse visits them and checks Tess. She reassures them everything is going as planned. It's only a matter of time!

An incubator helps keep babies warm after birth.

Getting ready for an operation

The operation room is where surgery takes place. But before an operation on a patient can begin, everyone must take great care to ensure that they are clean and wearing the correct clothes. There is a sink outside the operation room with powerful soap that kills many germs. Dr. Katherine washes her hands all the way down to her elbows. She thoroughly scrubs her fingertips and has soapy bubbles all over her arms. Then she uses warm water to wash away all the dirt and grime.

At the same time, Sarah, one of the assistants, ties the gown of her colleague Miguel. These gowns are designed to be worn only once. Sarah is excited—she enjoys performing surgery. It can be pretty stressful, but Sarah loves working with a large team of people to try to fix someone.

Hira is ready to be moved inside the operation room for an operation on a part of her body called the appendix, which is connected to her intestines. Hira's appendix is infected, and the surgeons have decided the best course of action is to remove it. Hira will be fine without it.

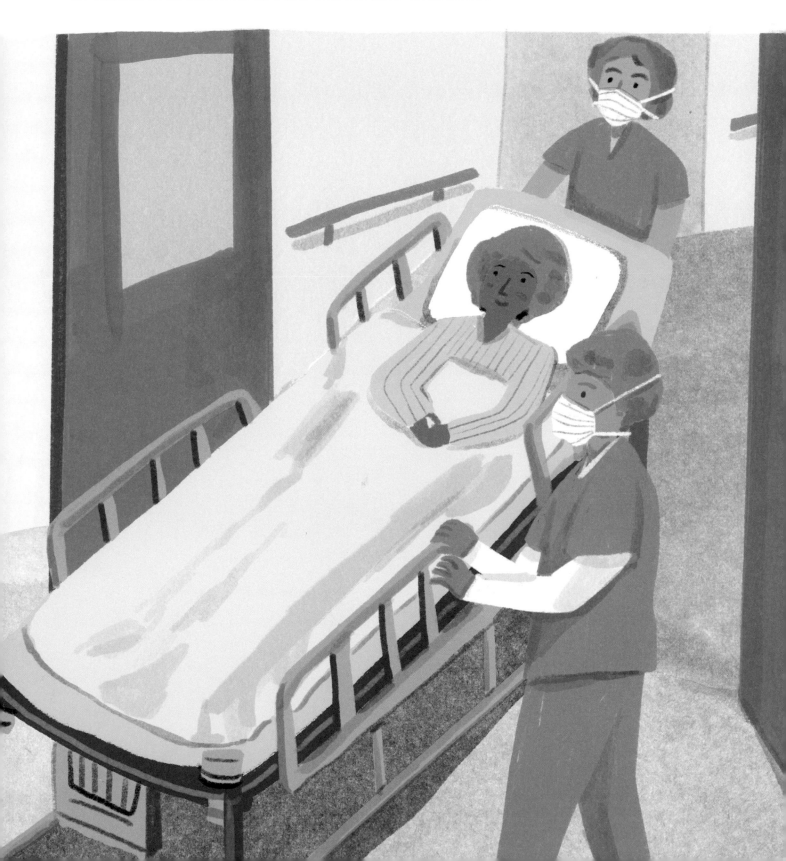

The operation room

It is time for Hira to have her operation. She has been moved into the operation room. This is a room in the hospital that has special equipment for going inside a patient's body in order to help heal them. It is a large room with plenty of space so the surgical team can easily move around the patient.

It's important the team can see the patients clearly, so the room is very well lit.

The monitor provides valuable information on how the patient is doing during the surgery.

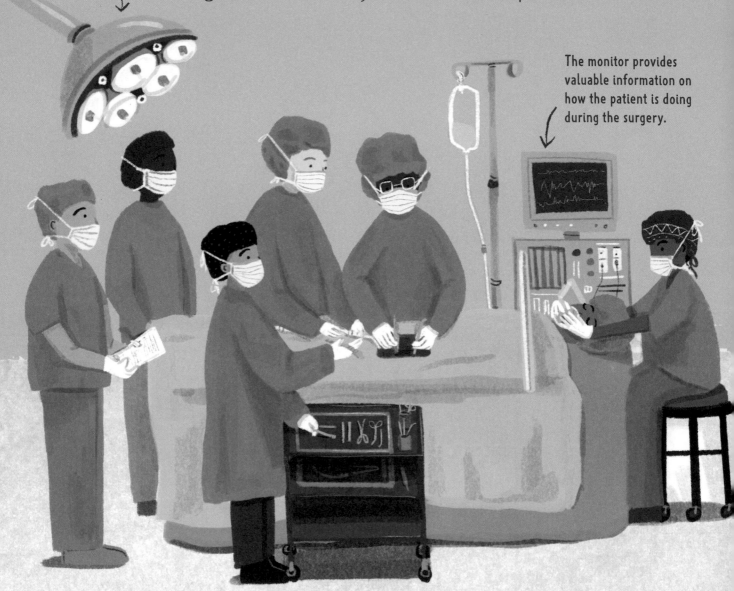

Having an operation

Hira is given a medication that will make her sleep through the operation— this means she won't feel any pain at all while it takes place. Dr. Katherine, who is in charge of the surgery, asks everyone to introduce themselves and explain their role in taking care of Hira. Then it's time to operate!

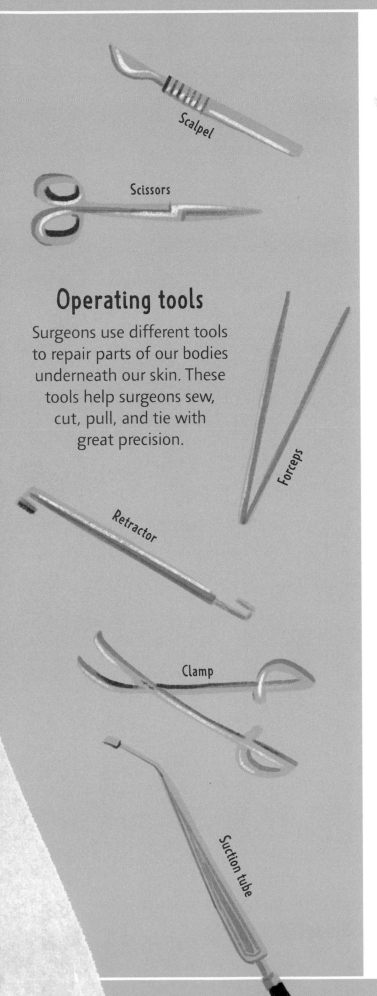

Operating tools

Surgeons use different tools to repair parts of our bodies underneath our skin. These tools help surgeons sew, cut, pull, and tie with great precision.

Scalpel

Scissors

Forceps

Retractor

Clamp

Suction tube

Surgeon
Surgeons are special doctors who fix things inside your body.

Anesthesiologist
These doctors make sure patients don't feel anything that happens during surgery.

Scrub tech
Scrub techs hand the surgeon the tools they need to perform the surgery.

Circulating nurse
Circulating nurses provide all the nursing care for the patient in the operation room.

First assistant and second assistant
The assistants are often doctors in training. They help the surgeon during the operation.

In the playroom

Tucked away in one corner of the hospital is a place reserved for special patients—the playroom. While most of the hospital is filled with doctors and nurses running around, the playroom is an oasis of calm just for kids.

Toby and Alejandrina are busy drawing at the table, while Pedro plays with building blocks. Receiving treatment at the hospital can be a little bit scary for some kids, but in here there is nothing to worry about. The playroom is packed with toys, games, paintbrushes, and pencils. Adults can enter, but they aren't allowed to talk about medications or surgery. They can only pick up a coloring book and join in the fun!

Child life specialists are trained to work with children in the hospital.

Physical therapy

David recently had surgery on his leg and it left him feeling weaker than before. His surgeon told him that he would work with Allister, the physical therapist at the hospital. Allister specializes in using exercise to strengthen muscles and help people recover from illness and injuries. It isn't easy for David to move his body when he feels so weak, but Allister is patient and kind. He demonstrates many of the exercises for David, and now he even has him running on a treadmill!

As a physical therapist, Allister also works with children. Some kids need help learning how to walk, while others work on improving their balance. Often the therapy sessions include fun games and activities.

In a room next door Pauline works with Dionne, the speech and language therapist, to improve her ability to talk. Pauline recently had a stroke, which makes it difficult for her to pronounce certain words. Dionne also uses a special exercise with apples to help Pauline swallow properly.

Meanwhile Jessica, the occupational therapist, uses a puzzle to help Alex improve his hand-eye coordination. Alex has noticed that ever since he started his sessions with Jessica it is easier for him to do things like catch a ball and write his name.

Ambulance to the rescue!

Kevin runs toward the merry-go-round the moment he and his mother arrive at the park. He feels like he can fly when he's spinning. He pumps his legs to go faster and faster, the park around him turning into a green blur. "Look at me, Mom!" he yells, as he starts to feel a bit dizzy.

Kevin lets go of the metal bar and flings his arms out. But the second he lets go he loses his balance. For a brief moment he really is flying! But then he crashes down hard on the ground. Kevin's mother runs to his side as he clasps his arm and starts to cry.

An onlooker who saw the accident calls 911, or the emergency services, and tells them what has happened. A few minutes later, the whole park can hear the sound of the ambulance's siren. Help has arrived!

Paramedics Glory and Niki introduce themselves to Kevin and his mom. They are trained professionals who provide medical care to people who are out and about. Both paramedics are concerned that Kevin may have broken his arm. It's important for him to see the doctors at the hospital. They put him in the ambulance and speed off.

Getting to the hospital

Paramedics have a crucial job. Not only do they need to get patients to a hospital as quickly as possible, they also have to take care of the patients on the way. Luckily ambulances are packed with amazing life-saving equipment.

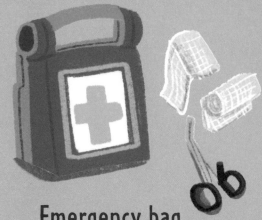

Emergency bag

An emergency bag holds important tools like bandages and scissors for paramedics to use when they arrive at the scene of an accident.

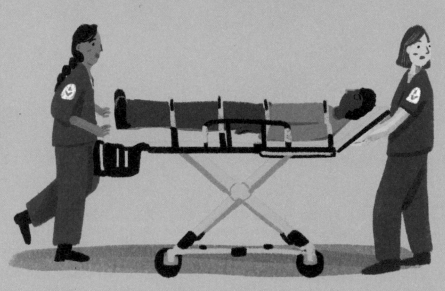

Stretcher

If you are hurt in an accident, paramedics will often use a stretcher to transport you to the ambulance. They are lightweight and easy to move around.

A neck brace holds your head and neck very still.

Backboard →

Safe and secure

The stretcher has belts to make sure that you are securely fastened to the backboard and won't fall off. This is to protect you from any further injury.

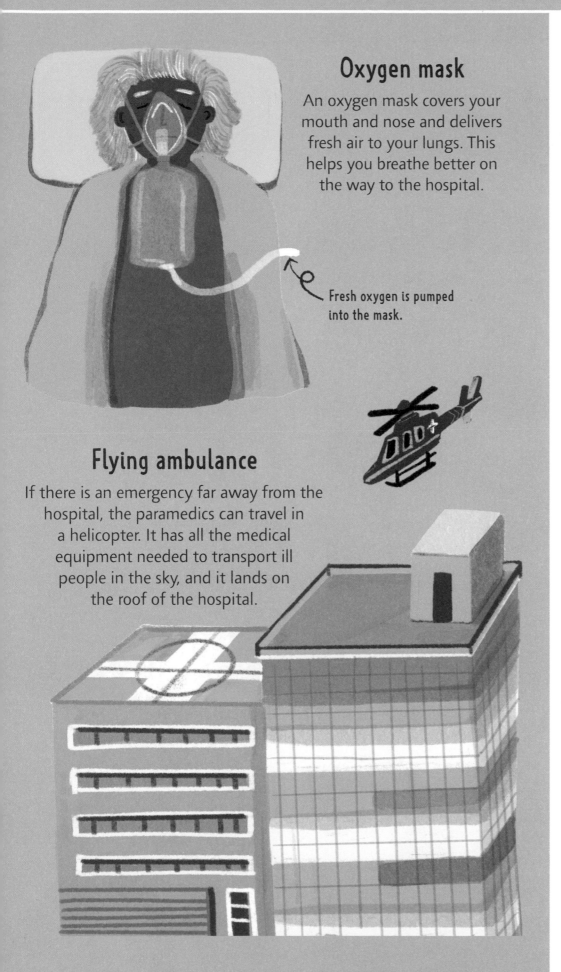

Oxygen mask

An oxygen mask covers your mouth and nose and delivers fresh air to your lungs. This helps you breathe better on the way to the hospital.

Fresh oxygen is pumped into the mask.

Flying ambulance

If there is an emergency far away from the hospital, the paramedics can travel in a helicopter. It has all the medical equipment needed to transport ill people in the sky, and it lands on the roof of the hospital.

Paramedics
Paramedics are medical experts who respond to emergencies in the community.

Dispatcher
The dispatcher responds to 911 calls. They organize which emergency services arrive to help a person in need.

Triage nurse
The triage nurse talks to the paramedics and decides where in the hospital the injured or unwell person will go.

The hustle and bustle of the ER

There is never a dull moment in the emergency room (ER). This is where people go when they do not feel well and need help right away. People come to the ER with all kinds of problems, like a tummy ache or a bad cut after a fall. When a patient arrives, a triage nurse first asks them how they are feeling and what kind of help they may need. This nurse helps figure out how serious the patient's issue is. This is important, because in the ER the most ill people get the most help first. With so many unwell and injured people around, it can feel overwhelming. But the people who work in the ER are used to working at great speed and under enormous pressure.

Unfortunately, Juan was in a car accident that left him severely injured. Paramedics Glory and Niki were the first responders to the scene of the accident and drove Juan to the hospital by ambulance. Now they've arrived in the emergency department, where Juan is being assessed by Dr. Lenny and Nurse Ashley.

They make a note of Juan's breathing, how quickly his heart is pumping, and if he has any big cuts or bruises. This information will help them better care for Juan and decide on the next course of action.

Down the hall, Nurse Paul is taking care of Roger, who fell over earlier in the day and hurt his right shoulder. His wife also noticed that Roger had a large gash across his forehead. At the hospital Roger's right arm has been put in a sling, and now he's about to get the cut stitched up. Stitches are threads that doctors use to help a wound heal. The doctor will bring the edges of Roger's cut together and use a special thread to help close the wound, like sewing two pieces of material together. Paul gets the stitching tray ready for the doctor, while Roger tries to make him laugh.

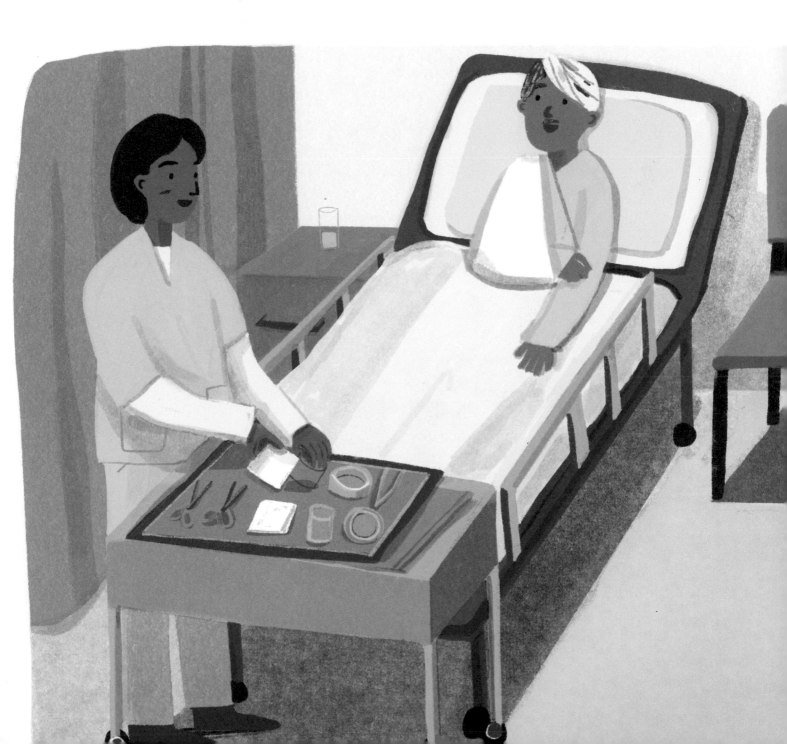

Getting an X-ray

The doctor calls Kevin and his mom into her office and looks at his arm. Kevin is being brave but Dr. Joan can tell he's not comfortable, so she gives him some medicine to help ease the pain. She tells him that she wants to X-ray his arm to see if any bones have broken. Kevin is led into a room and instructed to gently lay his arm flat on a table. A technician positions the X-ray machine before stepping outside the room while it works. A quick buzzing sound later and it's done.

X-ray machine

Everyone else waits outside.

Kevin keeps his arm as still as possible.

Once the X-ray comes through to Dr. Joan's machine, she goes over it with Kevin and his mom. She points to a small gray area.

"That there is a small fracture, I'm afraid," she says.

Kevin looks worried, then perks up. "Does this mean I get a cast?" he asks.

"It sure does!" says Dr. Joan.

Slowly and gently she cleans Kevin's arm, before winding a bandage around it. Dr. Joan asks Kevin what color cast he wants. He decides on blue. Dr. Joan dips a roll of material in some liquid and starts wrapping it over the bandage. Kevin then keeps very still while it dries.

The radiology department

Radiologists are doctors who use all sorts of cool machines to look inside your body. The images created help the medical team spot illnesses or find injuries. Radiologists use different machines to look at broken bones, check on babies who haven't been born yet, and make sure everything inside your body is working like it's supposed to.

X-ray

An X-ray machine uses energy waves to create images of the inside of your body. X-rays pass through your body, creating a picture. It's very safe and the result looks like an old black-and-white photo.

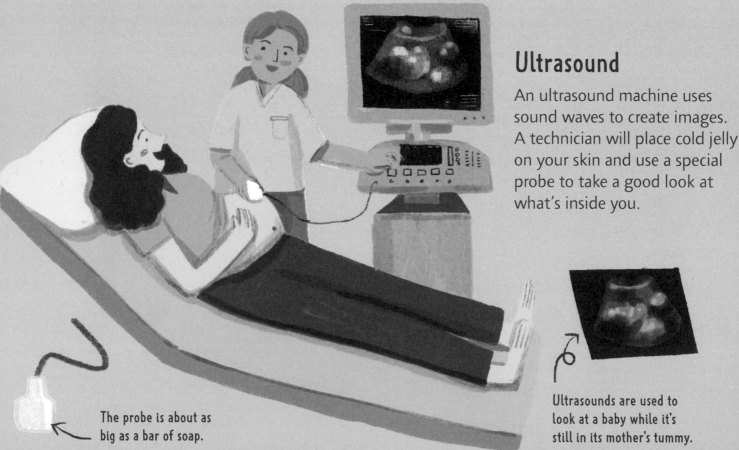

Ultrasound

An ultrasound machine uses sound waves to create images. A technician will place cold jelly on your skin and use a special probe to take a good look at what's inside you.

The probe is about as big as a bar of soap.

Ultrasounds are used to look at a baby while it's still in its mother's tummy.

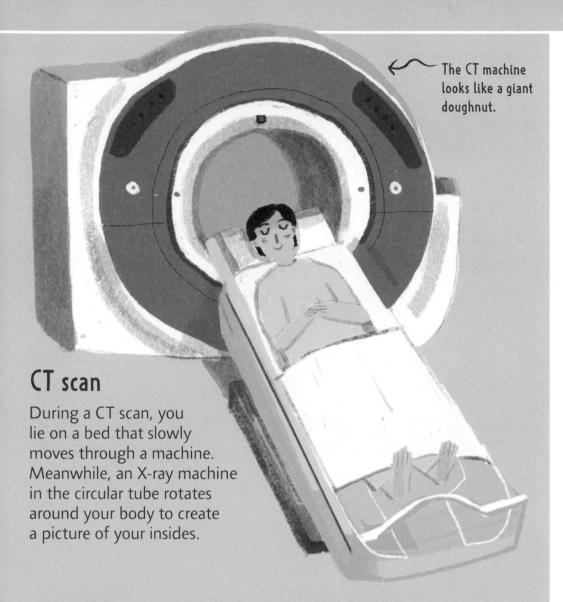

The CT machine looks like a giant doughnut.

CT scan

During a CT scan, you lie on a bed that slowly moves through a machine. Meanwhile, an X-ray machine in the circular tube rotates around your body to create a picture of your insides.

Viewing room

The images produced by the different machines in the radiology department are sent to the viewing room. A radiologist will look at all of the images and tell your doctor what the results are.

Radiologists

Radiologists are doctors who are trained to use medical images to find and treat injuries and diseases.

Technicians

Technicians operate the machinery to capture the images of your body.

Nurses

Radiology nurses look after the patients who come to the radiology department.

At the pharmacy

Jim has been feeling strange for a few days, ever since he lost the hearing in his right ear. He went to see a doctor who told him he has an ear infection. The doctor wrote Jim a prescription for some ear drops, which he will need to take twice a day for a few weeks. Medications come in all colors and types, from purple pills to blue inhalers and clear liquids. Jim arrives at the pharmacy in the hospital and gives Jenna the pharmacist his prescription form.

Pharmacists are healthcare professionals who study the effects of medicine on the human body. Jenna looks at Jim's prescription before going to the storage room to find the correct medication. As she hands it to Jim, Jenna explains it's important he uses the ear drops twice a day.

"If you don't do that, they might not be effective," Jenna warns.

Meet your little sister

The baby is here! After a grueling few hours giving birth, Tess holds her daughter tightly and watches her as she sleeps. Omari lifts up Michael so he can get a view of his new baby sister.

"How do you feel about being a big brother?" he asks.

The doctors and nurses have examined Tess and the baby. Both are healthy, happy, and tired. Dr. Holly was by Tess's side for the delivery and reminds the family that their new children's doctor will be in to visit soon to check on them. Before she goes, she asks Tess and Omari if they have a name for the baby yet.

"We've decided to call her Cherie," says Tess, smiling.

Intensive care

Amani sits with her mother as Dr. Amitte details her father's condition. He had been feeling ill for a few weeks, and when he went to the hospital, the doctors decided that he needed to be in the intensive care unit. In this part of the hospital his condition can be monitored at all times.

"I'm afraid that he is very ill and that he may not live long," explains Dr. Amitte.

Amani holds her mother's hand tighter and remembers when her grandfather died. She was scared then, and she feels the same way now. Her father is hooked up to several machines that are monitoring his breathing and his heart. He is receiving medication directly into his bloodstream through an IV line, and a device called a nasal cannula is helping him breathe through his nose.

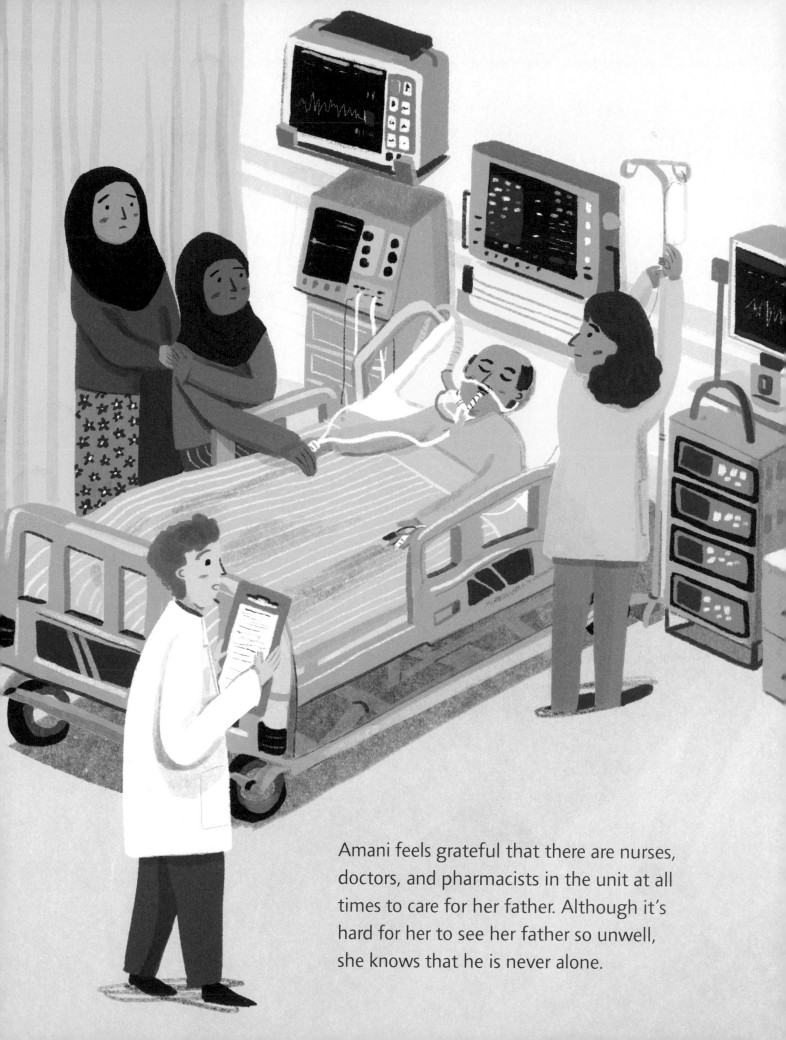

Amani feels grateful that there are nurses, doctors, and pharmacists in the unit at all times to care for her father. Although it's hard for her to see her father so unwell, she knows that he is never alone.

A team effort

I t takes a lot of people to make sure a community is healthy. When you enter the hospital or your local doctor's office, you will find that there are different types of people working together. Your doctor works with the nurses, pharmacists, and mental health professionals to make sure you get the right treatment. The social worker partners with community health workers to make sure you have a safe environment to live in. Everyone depends on one another—there is no way anyone can do it alone.

Life is tough and our emotions can be difficult to deal with. Mental health professionals give us ways to better understand and explore our feelings.

Social workers go out and about in the community to help people and families who are struggling. They let patients know about special programs that can help them— whatever situation they find themselves in.

Community health workers are trained volunteers from the local neighborhood. They work with health organizations to provide the best possible care for patients.

Doctors talk with the rest of the team to make sure patients are being looked after inside and outside the hospital. If they're ever unsure of anything they will talk it over with their colleagues. Together they can find solutions to almost anything.

The laundry room

In the basement of the hospital is a room filled with the smell of soap and the sound of whirring machines. This is the laundry room, and it's one of the most important places in the hospital. There are big washing and drying machines going all day long, while plenty of people are on hand to help sort the laundry into neat piles.

The team tell jokes and laugh as they complete their tasks, but this is serious work. The items cleaned in the laundry are delivered to all parts of the hospital so that patients have a warm blanket for bedtime or a new gown to change into after a shower.

Mopping the floor is Terry, one of the hospital's cleaners. Terry and his team have the important job of making sure the hospital is free of dirt and bacteria, creating a safe environment for the medical teams to work in.

Time for a break

Everyone deserves a break, especially when it involves muffins and coffee! In between the rush of seeing patients, members of the healthcare team visit the cafeteria in the afternoon to rest and chat with their colleagues. Doctors Wardah and Onyi discuss their kids and plans for the upcoming weekend. Meanwhile, Dr. Joanna runs into Pete the physical therapist, who is about to begin his shift. They haven't seen each other since Joanna started working in a new area of the hospital. She is impressed by Pete's new hairdo! With such busy and important jobs, the members of the hospital appreciate the valuable chance to recharge in the cafeteria before heading out again to look after their patients.

How's everyone doing?

Night starts to fall over the hospital, and for some patients it has been a very busy day. The hospital staff check in on them to see how they're doing. Pedro is looking forward to getting some sleep after a morning of cancer treatments and an exciting time in the playroom.

"You were very brave today, Pedro," says Dr. William at his bedside.

"Will you be back tomorrow?" asks Pedro, clasping his teddy bear.

"You bet," replies Dr. William.

David tells Dr. Christle about his first experience with physical therapy.

"I was a little nervous, but working with Allister on the treadmill I felt some of my strength coming back. He worked me hard, though!"

Dr. Christle laughs. "Just you wait until the next session," she says.

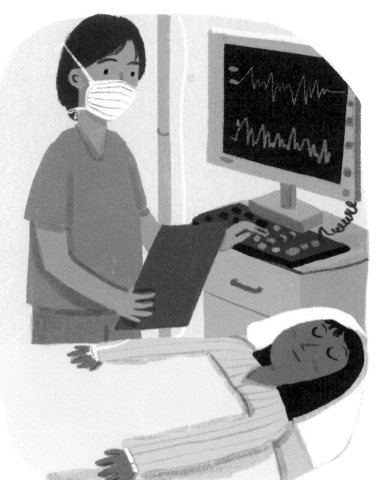

Hira's appendix surgery went well, and she has been wheeled into the post-surgical observation unit. This is where the nurses can keep an eye on her. Nurse Priscilla checks the medication Hira is on and glances at the monitor. Everything is looking nice and healthy. It won't be long before Hira wakes up and Nurse Priscilla can tell her the surgery was a success.

It's been a few hours since Lian had her blood taken by Maria the phlebotomist. Dr. Lindsay and the team have looked at the results of the blood test and they're happy with what they see. Dr. Lindsay has given Lian some medication that should make her feel better, and she tells Lian that she can now go home!

Goodnight

The sun has set on another busy day at the hospital. As the night shift team arrive they're met by tired doctors and nurses, who update them on what happened during the day. Some patients hurry home to make family dinners, while others arrive in preparation for tomorrow's surgery.

As the clock strikes ten o'clock, Tess and Omari make their way outside with Cherie. The hospital's pace starts to slow down for the evening. Patients get ready for bed and the healthcare team settle down to watch over them as they sleep. Everyone needs a chance to rest. But no matter the time, there will always be someone at the hospital who will be able to help you if you need it.

Glossary

Ambulance
A special vehicle that transports ill or injured patients to the hospital.

Anesthesiologist
A doctor who makes sure you are not awake during surgery.

Appendix
A small organ that is attached to your intestines and can sometimes become infected. Not everyone has one!

Depression
A medical condition where someone feels very low and sad, even when they try to be happy.

Doctor
A medical professional trained to look after unwell people. Doctors can diagnose problems and suggest treatment.

ER (Emergency Room)
The place where people first go when they feel very ill or are injured. The people who work in the ER will determine if they can help you there, or if you need to be admitted to a different part of the hospital.

Fracture
Another name for a broken bone.

Intestines
Organs inside your body that are located below your stomach. The intestines are part of the system that helps you digest food.

Laboratory
The part of the hospital equipped to run special tests on blood samples.

Labor
The process of giving birth to a baby.

Maternity ward
The place in the hospital where people who are about to have a baby stay.

Medical school
A professional school that trains doctors.

Medication
Pills, liquids, and powders designed to help treat a disease or make us feel better.

Mental health
This is how you feel, think, and behave! It is important to care for both your mental and physical health.

Midwife
A medical professional trained to look after expectant parents and babies during childbirth.

Muscles
Parts of our body that help us move, dance, and play!

Nurse
A medical professional trained to look after unwell people. Nurses work with doctors to help make people feel better.

Operation
The process of a surgeon fixing something inside your body. Also called surgery.

Paramedic
A medical professional who responds to medical emergencies outside of the hospital, often in an ambulance.

Physician
Another name for a doctor.

Psychiatrist
A doctor who specializes in caring for your mind and your emotions.

Stethoscope
A special tool that helps doctors listen to parts of the body.

Surgeon
A doctor who operates on people.

Index

A

ambulances 33, 34, 35
anesthesiologists 26, 27
appendix 25, 57
assistants 27

B

babies 46, 47
bandages 34, 41
beds 13
blood 13, 16, 17, 18, 19
blood pressure 13
blood vessels 18
bones 40, 41
breakfast 10, 11, 12
broken bones 7, 40, 41, 42

C

cafeteria 4, 11, 54, 55
carts 16, 18
casts 41
circulating nurses 27
clamps 27
cleaners 4, 52, 53
cleaning wipes 16
community health workers 51
CT scans 43

D

depression 21
dispatchers 35

doctors 12, 15, 16, 18, 19, 20, 21, 22, 24, 25, 28, 33, 38, 40, 41, 47, 48, 49, 50, 51, 54, 55, 56, 57, 58

drips 13

E

ear drops 44, 45
ear infection 44, 45
emergency bags 34
ER (emergency room) 36, 37, 38, 39

F

forceps 27
fractures 40, 41

G

games 28, 30
germs 24, 52, 53
GP clinic 20, 21
GPs 20, 21

H

heart 13, 38, 48
helicopters 35

I

incubators 23
intensive care unit 15, 48, 49
intestines 25
IV lines 13, 48, 49

K

kitchen 10

L

lab technicians 18, 19
labor 9, 22, 23, 46, 47
laboratory 16, 19
laundry room 52, 53
lungs 35

M

maternity ward 9, 15
medical school 5
mental health 21, 50, 51
mental health professionals 21, 50, 51
merry-go-round 32
microscopes 19
midwives 22
monitors 13, 26
muscles 30

This has been a
NEON 🦑 SQUID
production

Dedicated to my loving family and to my first healthcare hero, my mom. Thank you for always believing that my dreams could be reality.

Author: Dr. Christle Nwora

Illustrator: Ginnie Hsu

Consultant: Dr. C. Fielder Camm
US Editor: Allison Singer

Neon Squid would like to thank:

Georgina Coles for proofreading.

Copyright © 2022 St. Martin's Press
120 Broadway, New York, NY 10271

Created for St. Martin's Press
by Neon Squid
The Stables, 4 Crinan Street,
London, N1 9XW

EU representative: Macmillan Publishers Ireland Ltd,
1st Floor, The Liffey Trust Centre,
117-126 Sheriff Street Upper,
Dublin 1, D01 YC43

10 9 8 7 6 5 4 3 2 1

The right of Dr. Christle Nwora to be identified as the author of this work has been asserted in accordance with the Copyright, Designs and Patents Act, 1988.

Library of Congress Cataloging-in-Publication Data is available.

Printed and bound by Vivar Printing in Malaysia.

ISBN: 978-1-684-49204-6

Published in April 2022.

www.neonsquidbooks.com